Hummel
The Original Illustrations of Sister Maria Innocentia Hummel

9 8 7 6 5 4 3 2 1
Digit on the right indicates the number of this printing

ISBN 0-7624-0381-0

Library of Congress
Cataloging-in-Publication Number 98-70169

Author: Angelika Koller
Translation: William W. Bellis
Illustrations: Sister Maria Innocentia Hummel
Design: Eva Schindler

This book may be ordered by mail from the publisher.
But try your bookstore first!

Published by Courage Books, an imprint of
Running Press Book Publishers
125 South Twenty-second Street
Philadelphia, Pennsylvania 19103-4399

Angelika Koller

Hummel

The Original Illustrations of
Sister Maria Innocentia Hummel

COURAGE
BOOKS

an imprint of Running Press
Philadelphia · London

*If we but wholly would
be all that we should
T'would be the perfect
way to pray.*

M. Innocentia Hummel

Coquettes
H 308

An artist who became known throughout the world even though her most popular work was long not accepted by the critics; a gifted young woman who had to and knew how to assert herself among the academic art teachers of Munich, the metropolis of art; a girl from the country who missed her family back home; a student whose talent justified the highest hopes who, after receiving the best marks for her studies, retired behind convent walls, there finally to devote the major part of her creative and bodily strength to the painting of "charming" pictures with motifs from childhood – a not unusual fate, but a most unusual woman – for all this, artist and nun, child of nature and penetrating observer, was Berta Hummel, later the Franciscan nun Sister Maria Innocentia Hummel, with her whole soul.

Who then was Berta Hummel, the creator of the world famous Hummel figures? Closer observation provides surprising insights into her life and work.

Massing 1909-1926

Berta Hummel was born in Massing on May 21, 1909. "Where in the world is that?" many will probably ask. In lower Bavaria, today an hour by car from Munich. Ten steps from the "Fence at the End of the World" between the "townlet" where Johanna Spyris Heidi meets Peter, and St. Petersburg on the Mississippi, home of Tom Sawyer and Huckleberry Finn. Massing is a typical small town in Bavaria, like small towns anywhere, a place where children can take their first steps in life free and unfettered, in harmony with nature. The childhood spent in these surroundings unmistakably influenced the work of Berta Hummel.

In 1909 Massing was a market area where farmers transacted their business. Today the place is scarcely larger, but its look has changed.

*Berta Hummel's
parents' house in Massing*

There is an open-air village museum featuring old-style farms, a church with an altarpiece by M. I. Hummel, a street and an elementary school that have been named after her and a Berta Hummel museum worth seeing that is located in her parents' house, the aim of which is to give visitors a sense of the artist's surroundings in childhood and youth and, by means of a wealth of samples of her youthful works, to show the wide spectrum of the artist and the stages of her artistic development.

Berta Hummel's father, Adolf Hummel (1885-1953), was a businessman who served some years as mayor and took an interest in local and family history. Her mother, Viktoria (1885-1983), came from a prosperous family of farmers. Her family also included the sisters Katharina, Viktoria and Kreszentia, and the brothers Adolf and Franz Wilhelm. A veritable "nest of Hummels", as the artist herself called a drawing that she once offered in appreciation for a vacation. When grown-up she continued to find security in the family.

Berta's talent drew attention very early. No scrap of paper was safe from her; not newspapers, not business letters or statements. Many a father would have angrily turned this messy scrawler over his knee. Not Adolf Hummel, who as a young man would have gladly become a sculptor or wood carver but had had to take over his father's business. Now he encouraged his daughter's efforts as much as he could. For Christmas she received a painting kit which made her especially happy. When her father was at the front in World War I there was no letter to him that didn't include a drawing of Berta's. When he came back he went with his daughters Berta and Senta to paint outdoors.

Life began in earnest for Berta Hummel on May 1, 1915, when she entered the first grade of a school run by an order of teaching nuns, the so called "Arme Schulschwestern". On her first report card Berta was praised for being as lively as she was industrious, cheerful and sensitive. Her teacher recalled how, ever ready to change, she swiftly carried out the wishes of her schoolmates, drawing now a flower, now a colorful bird. They loved it when suddenly one of them recognized herself in a sketch. More and more often she heard the request "Come on, Bertel! Draw me!" Thus, drawing became Berta Hummel's personal language in which she sought to participate in the world.

In May 1921 she entered the Marienhöhe Institute, a boarding school for girls run by the Englische Fräulein in Simbach. At first the school cost thirty marks a month, a price her parents could easily afford. At the hight of the runaway inflation of the time, in September 1923, the cost climbed to one million marks per day. Then, in 1924, the nightmare ended, and fees became thirty marks a month again.

Here too, she received excellent grades. Along with art, Berta had a special interest in literature and with youthful creativity she expressed in her own medium the impressions made on her by her reading. Thus, in 1925-26, she produced a cycle of illustrations to Friedrich W. Weber's "Dreizehnlinden". Berta had reacted sensitively to the lyrical scenes and betrayed through her choice of motifs her longing for an altogether different landscape – for the sea, for the Unknown.

Viktoria Hummel reported that her daughter spent hours on end painting the mountains. Then a gradual change came about. Berta went beyond simple sketched portraits of schoolmates and little works of fantasy. Her father and mother proudly noted her daughter's progress and were therefore easily convinced by her teachers in Simbach that the right place for Berta after graduation would be an art school where her gifts could be appropriately developed.

As art historian Christiane Vielhaber stresses, in the twenties and thirties it was not at all taken for granted that a girl should get higher education, much less a girl from the country. In fact, the number of women students sank from 20,000 in 1926 to 6,000 in 1935. A so-called "pud-

Off to Town
H 303

Farewell
H 310

ding" diploma in home economics was usually considered good enough. Hardly eighteen, Berta Hummel took the train for Munich to take the entrance exams at the Academy of Applied Arts.

Munich 1927-1931

"Up to now I don't like being in Munich at all. I feel terribly lonely.", complained Berta Hummel to her parents after six days in the big city. She had, however, passed the entrance exam, for which she had had, among other things, to draw a sumptuous chair draped in brocade, and something original on the theme "Birthday". In no time at all she won recognition at the school and enthusiastically set herself further goals: a study trip following in Dürer's footsteps to Venice and Florence where she could examine the frescoes of Fra Angelico whom she admired all her life.

In the years 1928-30 the remarkable water-color "Lady in Red" was created. It wasn't a self-portrait, still it did express the mood of the student years. A young woman has her back turned to the viewer. Her red knee-length dress exudes joy of life; she is wearing elegant shoes as if she wanted to break into a flashy performance of one of the modish dances of the time – the Tango or the Charleston. Her bobbed hair had just become the fashion in 1928. A typical child of that age, yet you might encounter such today. She embodies the style of the twentieth century. What virtuosity and sensitivity in color, line and the woman's bearing!

All that Munich had to offer in art was incorporated into the program of the Academy. They visited the museums where the Bavarian kings had gathered together works of Rubens, Rembrandt, El Greco, Murillo, Altdorfer and Dürer. The face of the city reflected the taste of such princely patrons as Lenbach and Franz von Stuck; but had been affected too by modern trends such as that of the "Blaue Reiter" headed by Franz Marc, Expressionism or the Deutsche Werkbund. Teachers and students took study trips together in the neighborhood of Munich, or to Salzburg, Lindau or Garmisch in order to paint the changing light in the mountains or around Lake Constance.

With the other students she could enjoy what Munich offered in the way of culture. Exibitions, theater, concerts, films. "Munich shone", as Thomas Mann said. Not only did the Nobel prize winner live there, but also successful authors such as Lion Feuchtwanger, whose books sold into the millions in Germany and the United States. The latter wrote in his novel of 1930, "Success", that Munich "with its neighboring lakes and mountains, with its impressive collections, its light, comfortable architecture, with its Fasching and its festivals" had to be "the nation's most beautiful city". What more could a student of art want? With all that offered to her, she didn't squander her time. Professors and students, without exception, testified that her talent in every way equaled her eagerness to study, be it water-colors or oil paintings, be it collages, paintings of animals, landscapes or still lifes.

She was especially good at caricature. She had secretly drawn the professor Max Dasio (1865-1954) and done a wood carving which came indirectly to him and so captivated him that he invited Berta Hummel to paint him. This she did, going to Dasio in his studio where

The Runaway
H 218

he modeled for her while reading a newspaper and smoking a cigar. His satisfacion he expressed by a further invitation. "Come back if you have the yen to. I'm always around".

Most understandably, Berta promptly reported the event to her parents. The best of grades – and she only got A's – couldn't make clearer how highly this teacher prized her.

With the others, she got along marvelously, too. In Else Brauneis from whom she took

May You Sing
H 495

water color she found a companion. Else Braun-relations with most of Berta Hummel she felt her exceptionally intel- sympathetic motherly eis maintained friendly her women students. For great affection, found ligent and talented, yet there developed no special closeness between them. Berta Hummel's schedule left her no time; furthermore, students and teachers mostly discussed their subjects.

Otto Hufnagel, a fellow student, recalled: "She made a quick impression on fellow students and professors with her excellent sketching technique. She was quiet, very pretty and in my opinion a bit withdrawn from the social life that went along with school. Of course, this might have been due to her small-town background and the years she had spent away from home in strict religious schools; but at the same time she was clever and possessed a fantastic humor and quick wit that would pop up when you least expected it."

After eight semesters Berta Hummel passed the teachers' qualifying exams which tested her knowledge in such varied subjects as projection and figure drawing, colored sketches from nature, stylistics and art history. She got another A. She might have become a drawing teacher in an elementary school, any kind of girls' school or in teacher training programs. She might also have looked for a position as designer in commercial art or lived as a free-lance painter in Munich, Florence or Venice. Instead, she entered a convent.

Sießen 1931-1946

Entering a religious order strikes most people today as exotic. They know that in earlier centuries the surplus daughters of the rich and those of poor aristocrats, joined by simple girls from the people, who had neither dowry nor prospects of a husband nor means of maintaining an independent existence, entrusted themselves to the shelter of a convent. And yet, Francis of Assisi (1181-1226), founder of the Franciscan order, did in fact come from a merchant's family and could as easily have followed a worldly career rather than have responded as a young man to the call of Christ.

In Munich, Berta Hummel had met two Franciscan nuns from Sießen, Sr. M. Laura and Sr. M. Kostka, who lived with her in Maria-Theresien Student Residence in Blumenstraße and studied at the Academy of Applied Arts. For Berta Hummel there was no question about her wanting to live as an artist, but she felt increasingly the need to reconcile her faith with her art. Her encounter with Sr. M. Laura and Sr. M. Kostka played an important role in her decision to enter a convent. They were for her a concrete example that entering the convent didn't mean rejecting everything that one loved and cherished. Francis of Assisi had written and sung; these sisters painted and taught in schools.

Looked at as the child of her time and place, Berta Hummel appears as follows: she grew up in the neighborhood of a place of pilgrimage to Mary, Altötting, i. e. in the region where "Bavaria is at its most Catholic". Canonization proceedings made Konrad of Altötting, Bernadette Soubirous and Thomas Mores themes for conversation. Therese Neumann in Konnersreuth, a stigmatic since 1926, was revered by many. And not only the church cared about the cult of saints. Author Gertrud von Le Fort had success with her novel "The Song at the Scaffold", the story of a nun during the French Revolution, and Marc Chagall painted Biblical scenes. In 1926 there were in Germany 559 monasteries with 10,485 members and 6,619 convents with 73,880 members working in hospitals, schools and other areas of community service. Monks and nuns could be encountered in every area of life and were respected by everyone. Viewed thus, Berta Hum-

Francis of Assisi
H 670

Blessings
H 538

mel was not taking an unusual step. Parents and sisters were proud of her; only her brothers advised against it. These she quieted by saying jestingly to them that she couldn't find a husband superior to herself and was so bad at running a house that she needed the convent to look after her.

After applying on August 14, 1930 to be accepted in the convent at Sießen, she concluded her studies, allowed herself five weeks vacation and entered the convent as a novice on April 22, 1931. She quickly recognized that the reality of convent life was quite different from what she had imagined. Everything was new, unusual, strange, but she didn't let herself get discouraged. On August 22, 1933 she received the habit and took the name Maria Innocentia. On August 30, 1937 she made her final vows and promised to live forever in poverty, chastity and obedience.

The art critic Franz Thym observes: "If the look of the old photographs doesn't deceive, Berta Hummel must have been a pretty happy nun."

The convent at Sießen, situated near Saulgau in Württemberg and founded in 1259 by the knight Steinmar von Strahlegg, housed Dominican nuns for 550 years before it was purchased, after a fifty year intermission caused by the Napoleonic Secularization in 1803, by the Franciscans in 1860. In the early 1700's the church and some inner rooms had been constructed and partly restored by the brothers Dominikus and Johann Baptist Zimmermann. Along with a farm, a bakery for baking altar bread, a hospital, a children's home, and schools, the nuns had among their shops a parament shop in which cloths were fashioned for various uses in the sanctuary. From it came mass vestments, altar cloths and banners among other things.

When the trio from Munich – Berta, Laura and Cantalicia – came on the scene, the person in charge, Eligia Stadler, had great hopes that a new era in the art of clothmaking was about to begin. They initiated a new program, numbering from one and sweeping aside as kitsch all that they had produced before. Consequently, a priest expressed his gratitude, especially to Sister Innocentia. He rejoiced that his new, modern altar vestments complemented the beauty of the liturgy even though they had none of the conventional symbols.

Besides working in the parament shop, Berta spent one day a week teaching drawing at St. Anna school in Saulgau and designed pictures for various uses, such as prayer cards and Christmas, Easter or Communion cards. In 1933 Berta Hummel and the convent signed an agreement with the publisher of Ars Sacra in Munich, and in 1934 followed the association with W. Goebel Porzellanfabrik near Coburg. In 1935 she received permission to undertake two more years of art study in Munich, to prepare herself to meet all coming demands that might be made on her. The certificate for this work conferred on April 24, 1937 confirmed her artistic gifts anew.

This latest very good grade is noteworthy inasmuch as the "Hummel postcards" had at that point just been outlawed by the Nazi regime. Its party, seizing power, had taken a lot of people in by a show of friendliness toward the church, but once in control, had dropped its mask. Its aim was to drive the church out of public life and above all to make the education system a state monopoly. The totalitarian and inhuman demand of the dictatorship hidden behind these actions is unmistakably clear in the motto of the Hitler youth "Whoever on the flag of the Führer swears keeps nothing personal that he bears" – not even himself or his belief in God.

In 1935 more than seven hundred priests unacceptable to the regime were arrested and many educational institutions of the church were closed, among them the private teacher training program in Sießen. In 1937, after the papal address to the German people formulated by Munich's Cardinal

The convent of Sießen near Saulgau

Berta Hummel with her family, on 4th June 1933

Faulhaber for Pope der Sorge", an attack had been allowed to pit, the Nazi regime Pius XI, "Mit brennen- on the Nazi regime, be read from the pul- cracked down harder.

Sießen was also affected. The schools of the order were closed and at the same time nuns were excluded by law from the state school system. Being forbidden to teach, they found the basis of their existence undermined, while at the same time their taxes were increased.

In 1940, the Nazis requisitioned the convent buildings to provide shelter for twelve hundred ethnic Germans from Romania. Two hundred fifty nuns had to leave the convent. Berta Hummel went first to stay at her parent's house but a few weeks later returned to Sießen. From the beginning she had contributed to the support of the convent with her paintings and publications and now was among the forty nuns who held out and worked tirelessly in spite of all reprisals. Her deepest wish then was: "Let freedom come soon – even if we have to start all over again at the beginning". Yet, in spite of everything, she described herself as "perfectly happy" (June 9, 1944). She had found the meaning of her life in the convent.

Berta Hummel's health had always been delicate. As a student, she had found the long art exams "physically very exhausting". At the convent in Sießen they had taken care that she not push herself too hard, but the physical deprivations and the psychic horrors of the years of terror were finally too much.

In August 1944, Berta Hummel fell ill with pleurisy and spent the winter in the Wilhelmstift sanatorium in Isny in Allgäu, a region in southern Bavaria. In April 1945, apparently cured, she returned to Sießen at her own request. But by July she fell ill again. In the middle of September 1945 she was transferred to the sanatorium in Wangen, also in Allgäu, where she was diagnosed as having tuberculosis with bleeding in the lungs.

The people around her tried to help as much as possible, the publisher of Ars Sacra even trying to make it possible for Sister M. I. Hummel to travel to Switzerland for treatment. He obtained permissions and a Visa, and an American major even offered to arrange a medical evacuation flight to Switzerland for the patient, but, considering her poor condition, the doctors advised against it.

In Wangen, until spring 1946 she recuperated to the point of being able to paint again and by June she had created some small works which after her death were published by Fink publishing house in Stuttgart under the title "Last Gifts".

At the beginning of September she went back to Sießen, but her condition remained delicate. At the end of October another relapse occurred. In the company of members of the order and her mother Sister M. I. Hummel died in the convent on November 6, 1946.

Shortly before her death, Sister Maria Innocentia Hummel had said that she was only the "little brush" waiting for the master whose hand would take it up to create joy or toss it aside. She looked upon herself as an instrument, sought no fame and continued the tradition of a serving art that had existed since the Middle Ages and was the very antithesis of the modern notion of genius which places the person of the artist above the work. How much Sister M. Innocentia Hummel as a person stayed in the background of her work is made clear by a convent anecdote: visitors to Sießen were amiably and compentently led by a nun through the Hummel room, neither told, nor suspecting that it was the artist herself serving as guide.

Berta Hummel was made famous by her figures of children which delighted a wide public, though they drew fire from art critics. The Bishop of Regensburg, Michael Buchberger, himself knowledgeable about art, warned after the appearance of the Stuttgart Hummel book in 1934 that she needed "a great and serious task so that she can grow intellectually, spiritually and artistically."

Such a challenge was to portray the Passion of Christ.

In 1934 Berta Hummel said guardedly that she was thinking about painting a Way of the Cross, but didn't think herself at that point adequately prepared. Then, during her second period of study in Munich, she began a Way of the Cross cycle which has since come to be recognized as a key work and as her most significant contribution to sacred art. Fully consistent in themselves, the paintings make no concession whatso-ever to the public's taste. For a long time they remained in the archives in Sießen till in the seventies peo-ple there recognized the value of her work.

Berta Hummel's complete work con-sists of some six hun-dred paintings and drawings from her childhood, adoles-cence and student days, as well as

Sister M. Innocentia with children in the convent garden

16

Nature's Child
H 107

around five to seven hundred works from the convent period. The works are to be found partly in the hands of her family or private collectors and partly in Sießen. In Sießen too, there is to be found a catalogue of M. I. Hummel works begun by the artist and continued by Sister M. Laura.

The artist's signatures help to date her work: one finds first "Bertl Hummel", "B: Hummel" or "B. H.", then, after her name change in the convent, "M. I. Hummel" or simply "Hummel". However, if one observes her paintings closely, then a sort of "second signature", appears again and again in the form of her heraldic animal, a flying bumble-bee (which is, in German, a "hummel").

The complete works have sometimes been divided into three groups: first, landscapes, portraits and other non-religious motifs; second, religious works; third, Hummel children. This three-part division follows external criteria. But in fact, children with the typical Hummel face look out at us from religious works too, and many Hummel paintings in her series of children are genuine portraits or developed from them. Furthermore, Hummel children do not "live in a vacuum", for one frequently finds bits of alpine landscape in the background. Religious tradition is part of their life, and their relation to people, animals and plants manifests the Franciscan ideal of the child of God.

Another division of her work would be what she chose and what she was commissioned to do. What came simply from within her and what resulted from the influence of others? Work of her own choosing was done mostly in childhood and adolescence. In her student years the greater part was done to meet the requirements of the academic curriculum. What she produced during her convent years frequently fulfilled requests put in by the convent workshops, by Ars Sacra or the W. Goebel Porzellanfabrik.

Now and again she may have yearned for more freedom. Yet she sometimes groaned that she wasn't really very pious and still had to

Cinderella
H 154

produce a lot of pious paintings. Occasionally she felt herself hemmed in by the habit she wore. On a visit to Freiburg she was enchanted by its old narrow streets and their strange angles but considered it inappropriate for a nun to be painting out-of-doors. Such signs of regret don't go so far as to suggest that Sister M. Innocentia Hummel preferred works of her own imagination and choosing. Without a doubt she did take pleasure in her paintings of children.

When Berta Hummel made concessions to those commissioning her work, such concessions touched on themes, choice and number of motifs, format. Never on the quality.

At the beginning of her work with Ars Sacra she first sent the publisher large-sized originals in varying formats, a practice which made both setting copy and sending through the mail difficult. An agreement was therefore reached, whereby prints from photographs of the large-sized sketches were first to be sent to Ars Sacra for selection and the selection to be sent back to Sister Maria Innocentia to re-do in color in small format. The publisher wanted about forty new motifs a year, most of them worldly, only a few religious ... And with the worldly motifs went also the annual demands for fresh cards from the artist for Christmas, New Year and Easter.

How seriously she reflected on the creation of her works can be seen by a glimpse at her correspondence with the art professor, Kurz, during her work on Our Lady of Perpetual Help for Ratmannsdorf. "I have honestly striven to take your wishes and ideas into account. ... as for myself. I would much prefer not to do angels. To avoid the danger of trivialization for one thing and above all to restrict the idea and composition of the painting to the essential. On these grounds also I diapprove of clusters of figures. They make it too easy to sum everything up, something which mostly doesn't signify improvement." (July 8, 1940).

Berta Hummel was first and foremost a painter, not a printer or sculptress, yet she did attend seriously to the reproduction of her work. The W. Goebel Porzellanfabrik worked a long time until the best manufacturing process for the Hummel figurines was found. Usually a model was taken apart by cleanly cutting it into individual pieces so that afterwards a mold could be made. If the pieces of a figurine moved when being fit together and a boy's head sat crookedly on his shoulders then the whole impression of the original was distorted. So new tools and techniques of cutting were devised till they produced figurines of a quality which measured up to the highest artistic and technical standard.

Also in the beginning of her cooperation with Ars Sacra, the artist complained that, due to a new techique of printing, the colors of the reproductions were too loud, and were not the subdued tones of the originals. After several futile attempts with the not yet fully developed offset technique, the publisher went back to using the old method.

Hummel Books

In 1934, in an edition of five thousand copies, the Stuttgart publisher, Fink Verlag, brought out "The Hummel Book" with poems by the Viennese writer Margarete Seemann. The same author was also to write texts for a volume plan-ned by Ars Sacra, but she became so seriously ill that her responsibities were taken over by the Munich writer Joseph Bernhart (1881-1969).

On the Other Side
H 153

Following the maxim "Good things take time", Ars Sacra bided its time. It planned a volume that would bring together the best of Berta Hummel's creative work, and its publisher, Maximiliane Müller, provided the stimulus by visiting the painter several times and working together

Volunteers
H 655

with her on the book. Joseph Bernhart exercised critical influence. He chose the book's title, "Hui, die Hummel" (Here Comes the Bee), a pun on the painter's name, and he insisted that religious motifs be excluded so that the book wouldn' be a "hermaphrodite" and the critics wouldn't get the idea that it offered too few secular paintings.

The political situation hindered the spread of Berta Hummel's work for the Nazis felt that her angels and children were provocations. In 1937 the newspaper "The SA-Man" accused her of disparaging the nation's youth with her "hydrocephalic and club-footed goblins". The magazine "Hochland" spoke of "heresy". But it didn't stop with verbal attacks. Censorship measures began with a notice to businesses to stop displaying angels. Then the paper ration was cut and finally the distribution within Germany of all Hummel works was prohibited. Hummel works could be shipped abroad though – the dictatorship needed foreign exchange desperately. Ars Sacra was often searched. Books of various authors were confiscated and burned.

After Josef Müller, founder of the publishing house Ars Sacra, had died in 1935, his widow, Maximiliane Müller, and her son-in-law, Herbert Dubler, carried on his work. "When I bring out something" promised Dubler, "I'll back it to the limit that I have to." Dubler set himself on the side of the artist against the "anti-Hummel wind". "Hui, die Hummel" was brought out as late as 1939, and in 1940 John O. Riedl, a professor at Marquette University in Milwaukee sought translation rights for an American edition. In the worsening international situation of the spreading war, however, nothing further occurred.

The Hummel Figurines

In Advent 1933, Franz Goebel, co-owner of the W. Goebel Porzellanfabrik near Coburg, had traveled to Munich to make contact with potential customers and as a result came across postcards with Hummel motifs. Love at first sight led to a contract with the artist in 1934.

The sculptors Reinhold Unger (1880-1974) and Arthur Möller (1886-1972) devoted all their energies to develop the three-dimensional models for the later Hummel figurines from the two dimensions of the paintings. As early as 1935 the first collection was displayed at the Leipzig trade fair and immediately made a hit in America where the film career of child star Shirley Temple was beginning.

When Berta Hummel visited the Goebel plant in 1936 she was enthusiastically greeted by the workers and thanked by them for her part in their prosperity – which the war would interrupt but not end. The very first GI's who came to Germany swapped cigarettes and canned goods for Hummel figurines. Former First Lady, Betty Ford, owns a cabinet full of them. President Ronald Reagan received a gift of the Quartett of Singers on his visit to Bonn.

With the passing of years the widespread popular effect of Berta Hummel's work has become manifest in many ways. There is a club for passionate collectors. There are a number of museums, among them the one in New Braunfels, Texas, which houses the world's largest collection of original pictures by the artist as well as the Hummel-Saal in Sießen. Festivals are held annually. The "International M. I. Hummel Club", founded in North America in 1977, under the name "Goebel Collectors' Club" has grown to some 200,000 members in the U.S. and more than 60,000 in Europe. In the U.S. more than 30,000 people attend the festivals, held every year in a different state. Here Hummel figurines are swapped and sold and children compete in Look-alike-contests for prizes a-warded to those children who most resemble a particular figure.

Today almost every second German home possesses a Hummel figurine, even though these cost, depending on size, between 160 and 20,000 Deutschmarks. To think they

The Hummel Museum in New Braunfels, Texas

started in 1934 at four marks a piece! From the more than two hundred million mark yearly turnover for the manufacturer in Coburg are paid the salaries of up to two thousand specialists; from licenses flow high profits to the Franciscan Sisters and their missions.

The Hummel Children and the Art Critics

Considering the facts and figurines cited one must account the Hummel children an astonishing phenomenon, as tiny monuments of the twentieth century, not to be deprived of their place in cultural and social history. One may, of course, cry "Kitsch!" But what is kitsch exactly?

Kitsch is, one may say, something too nice, too sweet, too cute in comparison with things as one usually finds them, something that pops up everywhere, becomes so usual, that it stops being noticed. With such a definition mightn't one say that Picsso's endlessly reproduced "Child with the Dove" is also an instance of kitsch?

Some things that stem from Berta Hummel's workshop, no doubt, do deserve to be called kitsch. Some. Not all. What's more, no artist always turns out the best that is in him and especially not when pressed by deadlines. Reassessments made today will range some things of hers with folk art, which has of late become more highly valued than previously.

One does not, seriously, suggest comparing Hummel's forms of artistic expression with paintings by Kokoschka or Max Ernst. They are much too different. Still that all three of them were proscribed by the Nazis has to give one pause. All were condemned for their "degenerate art" for art having a humanistic side, striving toward freedom, upholding the value of feelings, the limits and the worth of the human being. In folk art

Hard Letters
H 622

Max and Morltz
H 352

and useful art too are rate these same high hu- of Berta Hummel's pain- them. works which incorpo- man values, and many tings belong among

In no way do all the Hummel children correspond to the type "nice and sweet". Many are sweet and gentle, fragile and dreamy; others, robust and impudent, appealing rascals who know their own mind. The whole range of their individuality can sometimes be observed in one to eight year olds in a swimming pool or at a kindergarten outing.

Berta Hummel does take her colors now and again from her pot of pastels, but she also consciously composes paintings in autumn tones or in more cheerful colors which make one reflect on the transitoriness of childhood and the child's need for protection. Over and over again irritating details find their way into her pictures, a cactus as mirror image, an angry snorting nose, exaggerated caricatures of the chubby-cheeked type.

In very many pictures Berta Hummel shows us children as they look in real life. In numerous others she bewitches us with fairy tale forms. Children symbolize in her work the ideals that children from time immemorial have represented: joy in life, innocence, love. In many pictures she holds a mirror up to grownups, and we encounter humorously critical caricatures.

In conclusion one may well cite the judgement on Berta Hummel's pictures of children by the art historian Ulrich Gertz who sensitively perceives the uniqueness of these works: "The key to the widespread effects of the artist is the universality of the child and the free spirit that we all had as children, and which now lies hidden deep inside us. Sister Maria Innocentia's handling of colors, feelings and gestures is thoroughly classical. If we were to seal her works up in a chest for a hundred years and then open it, her paintings would still be as strong and valuable as they are today."

Whoever owns this book doesn't have to wait a hundred years. Whoever till now hasn't taken notice of these pictures may now give them wholeharted attention.

What Is More Wonderful Than to Bring Joy to One's Fellowmen

Early Pictures for Ars Sacra
1933-1934

As a drawing teacher in Saulgau Berta Hummel rewarded hardworking pupils with religious pictures she had painted herself, and which had been printed by a small religious publisher named Ver Sacrum in Rottenburg. As it became clear that only a larger publisher could enable the artist to achieve the widespread impact she deserved, a priest advised her to submit a selection of her small compositions to the publisher Ars Sacra. Following his advice, Sister Eligia Stadler sent them three copies of drafts by Berta Hummel on March 9, 1933. The publisher, Josef Müller, recognized the quality of the pictures and promptly acquired the rights to them.

Some of those early Hummel pictures are included in this chapter.

Still predominant are individual figures and muted colors wherein one can hardly distinguish child from angel, and some pictures even remind one of silhouettes or give an impression of being surrounded by invisible frames in which the figure sits, trunk erect, like a doll or a bookend. But much that is typical of later mature work is there: side views for example or subtly differentiated gestures, pictures in pairs – boy and girl, child and angel – facing one another like mirror images. Important motifs show themselves already: country clothing and disheveled hair, birds as companions, astonished eyes, delight in music, love of travel and industriousness at work. These children are as much in need of protection as they are disposed to give things away.

Hello from me, you splendid May,
Sprouting and blooming in every way.

Wilhelm Busch

The Runaway
H 218

Were I but a little bird,
Oh how happily would I fly,
By no bird hindered in the sky ...

His Happy Pastime
H 305

... If I'm truly such a bird,
Then I may reach for everything,
On cherries snack while on the wing.

Friedrich Schlegel

Her Happy Pastime
H 306

Within my little room
I feel that time just crawls.
A boy sunk deep in gloom,
I'll soon be climbing walls.

Christian Adolf Overbeck

The Draftsman
H 262

Chimney Sweep
H 261

Off to Town
H 303

Looks Like Rain
H 304

Take a look at the earth!
It shouldn't be so.
And were we of more worth
It wouldn't be so.

Christian Adolf Overbeck

Little Nurse
H 660

The Golden Rule
H 166

Baby and the Bee
H 110

Alleluja
H 385

Sweet you smell dear little flower,
Truly sprung from Adam's bower! ...

Begging His Share
H 355

... Everywhere where angels go
A paradise is sure to grow.

Johann Martin Miller

Angel and Birds
H 454

You cities have most everything
Credit, money and golden ring,
But alders, oaks and other trees,
You've nothing to compare with these!
So has kind nature in her way
Us farmer folk sought to repay.

Matthias Claudius

Those Were Wonderful Days at Home

Life in the Country

After Berta Hummel had spent some days on vacation in Massing in 1942, she wrote to her family: "Those were wonderful days at home! May God bless you for all your love and kindness." The experience of those days and recollections of her childhood in Massing suggested pictures of children from everyday rural life.

Life in the country is regulated by the sequences of nature, the family and going to school. Compositions filled with figurines show the child as a social being in a world of parent, grandparents, brothers, sisters and schoolmates.

In the country the child moves about in the world of nature which simply does not exist for the child in the city. The contact with nature means among other things accepting responsibility, for it goes without saying that children in the country have chores, such as tending animals.

Berta Hummel here presents social reality; however, her reality looks quite different from that of Heinrich Zille and Käthe Kollwitz in whose pictures are seen neglected workers' children from the impoverished areas of big cities. While Kollwitz's and Zille's children are symbols of betrayed innocence, those of Berta Hummel experience the love of patient parents and grandparents and as a consequence possess and radiate a capacity to love. They embody the ideal of Franciscan childlikeness which relates not just to people but to animals as well. Francis of Assisi preached to the birds; Berta Hummel's little shepherd plays the flute for his lamb.

Be not the child of the whole big earth,
Be the child of the land of your birth.
And there make up your berth.

Knut Hamsun

Ring Around the Rosie
H 204

Children and clocks
shouldn't be repeatedly checked.
You must let them run too.

Jean Paul

And One Makes a Dozen
H 381

Love is the creator and ruler of all things.

Ernst Moritz Arndt

Playmates
H 372

Chick Girl
H 371

Return to the Fold
H 382

We should take less trouble
to prepare the way for our children
than our children for the way.

Saying from the U.S.

School Girls
H 197

School Boys
H 198

School Chums
H 194

What's that you say? Do I hear right?
The stork did bring a boy last night?
Most silently let's tiptoe in
Where sleeps our newest next-of-kin.

Youth Calendar 1851

Blessed Event
H 102

A father's goodness
reaches higher than a mountain, ...

The Work Is Done
H 313

*... a mother's goodness
is deeper than the sea.*

Japanese saying

Homeward Bound
H 314

Nothing's more lovable than your child's child.

Old German saying

Grandma's Story
H 151

Not in luck resides joy
But in joy luck.

Russian saying

Grandpa's Helper
H 152

The children tore their way through golden rods, asters, and cat tails to a little elevated spot.

"No, indeed, Tina: we are safe now", said Harry.

"Why don't you call me Grettel? We will play be Hensel and Grettel; and who knows what luck will come to us?"

Harriet Beecher Stowe: Oldtown Folks

Hansel and Gretel

Pairs of Children
Straight from Fairy Land

Should you look for Berta Hummel's models, you may well find them in the Alte Pinakothek in Munich, in such paintings by Murillo (1618-1682) as "Boys Playing Dice" and "The Little Vegetable Dealer". Like Murillo she frequently used muted but nontheless rich colors; as in his works so in hers, brown tones often predominate. Her teacher too, Max Dasio, did portraits of his daughters and grandchildren, posters for Help-the-Children Day, and allegoric representations, and possible models or parallels are to be found among Hermann Kaulbach, Hans Thoma, Ludwig Richter, Norman Rockwell, Grandma Moses and Andrew Wyeth.

It wasn't, however, just works of art that inspired Berta Hummel. Fairy tales, folk songs and children's books did too. Sometimes the title of a picture refers directly to a fairy tale, as in Hansel and Gretel; at other times the observer may let his fantasy run free. Are not these rough-pleasant farm children looking triumphantly and joyfully out of the window Hansel and Gretel after their victory over the witch? Isn't the Peter of Heidi's "townlet" laughing at us through them?

"Baby Brother and Baby Sister", taken also from the brothers Grimm, are depicted sometimes apart, sometimes as a pair. Typical for Berta Hummel's style, the composition is thus oriented symmetrically along a vertical axis. The motifs H 299 and H 300 show the mirror image character especially well.

*And since they needn't fear any longer,
they went into the gingerbread house
to search through everything.*

Hansel and Gretel by Grimm

Vacation Time
H 206

Beyond all care and mourning,
On high I viewed the land ...

Morning Light
H 122

...Where full many a good morning
Lay fresh and fair at hand.

Joseph von Eichendorff

Apple TreeGirl
H 298

Apple Tree Boy
H 297

For Mother
H 301

For Father
H 302

Peter collected the goats in the village every morning
to drive them up to the pasture where they
would be able to feed on the rich grass till evening. ...

The Little Goat Herder
H 235

*...Then Peter trooped down again
with the animals and when he came to the village
gave a shrill whistle through his fingers.*

Johanna Spyri: Heidi

The Goat Girl
H 205

Feeding Time
H 236

Girl on a Fence/I
H 299

Boy on a Fence
H 300

The eye of a child, a day in May,
We count as gifts from heaven;
And such that of them we may say
Eternity they'll leaven.

Folk Saying

Good Weather
and Bad Weather

HAB SONNE IM HERZEN OB'S STÜRMT
ODER SCHNEIT. OB DER HIMMEL VOLL
WOLKEN DIE ERDE VOLL STREIT

Children's Games

Many Hummel children play in an atmosphere that offers both protection and freedom. They don't at all need the many expensive toys which clutter children's lives today. A bird, an animal, a flower, the weather, a doll, and, above all, other children do very well for them.

Berta Hummel delineates the facial expression and the gestures of children with precision, from amazed reverence and quiet concern to bubbling joy in the world. She lets us in on the secrets of mischievous rascals. Her symbolic language is simple and clear. The bird shows the child what freedom is; the flower stands for life bursting into bloom. The umbrella symbolizes security; it protects against any kind of weather, real storms and political storms. It's curious that for "Good Weather" and "Stormy Weather" no verse occurred to Joseph Bernhart. Did he perhaps worry that the Nazis, sensing treason everywhere, could read even these pictures as attacks? Might they not think these children were saying, "The political weather is still good but we don't trust it and we are putting up our umbrellas! Politics may storm all it wants, but we'll survive under our umbrellas!"?

However that may be, through the happy expression of untroubled playing children, Berta Hummel, not least of all, fulfilled the wish of many buyers in whose name her publisher, Maximiliane Müller, spoke when she expressed thanks for some new motifs by the artist: "In today's sad times people yearn for an amusing Hummel card which can draw a joyful smile even from the dejected. You do so much good with your cards!"

The present is the only time
which does in truth belong to us,
and we must use it in
accordance with God's will.

Blaise Pascal

Not for You!
H 292

Who went about in youth complaining
Amidst the lustrous greens of spring?...

Friend of the Flowers
H 113

The Opinion/II
H 178

Blue Belle
H 209

Kiss Me
H 231

...Who isn't all complaint disdaining
While flowers bloom and voices sing?

After Ludwig Hölty

Max and Moritz
H 352

Sunny Weather
H 287

... The way you look at it
Will make it cheery or blue.

Friedrich Rückert

Stormy Weather
H 288

Have the sun in your heart
If it storms or snows,
If the heavens are cloudy,
The earth come to blows!...

Have the Sun in Your Heart
H 294

Umbrella Girl
H 296

Summertime
H 162

Slumber Time
H 120

… Have the sun in your heart
And let come what may!
You'll be flooded with light
On the darkest day! …

Follow the Leader
H 351

... Have a song on your lips;
Do not ever despair!
Have the sun in your heart,
And the weather'll be fair!

Cäsar Flaischlen

The Mountaineer
H 203

Out of Tune
H 141

Young Crawler
H 143

Coquettes
H 308

The sunshine in our life
Is song and joy without strife.

Proverb

Telling Her Secret
H 291

Two lads who'd gone out walking,
Before a ditch stood gawking.
The first leapt over, springing,
And landed almost singing,
"Ain't that finesse?"
The second, after thinking,
Sprang off but soon was sinking
Deep down in mess.

Wilhelm Busch

Adventure Bound

Exciting Experiences and
Dangers in Everyday Life

From a child's perspective there lie waiting in the world adventures and dangers which seem trivial and amusing to grownups but in truth can be keenly exciting or threatening. And what adult doesn't also tremble when he goes to the dentist?

Let an animal appear and the child goes weak. Except the bumble-bee, flitting through the child's world as the artist's heraldic animal. The child is occasionally the "eighth Swabian" from the fairy tale expecting dragons where there are only rabbits.

Fences are great things there. They protect from feathered and four-legged creatures and do much more besides. In fact they may well be the most many-sided symbols in Berta Hummel's paintings; standing behind one, the child is as if shut out, denied particular experiences. Sitting on one, the child has the impression of being secure or triumphant, king of the fence because he has conquered a piece of the world.

Opposed to little scaredy-cats are the brave children, singing and hiking through the world. Boldly they take hold of a jar of honey, and they hang on to it in spite of stinging competition. Modern life too, camera technique and skiing, finds a way into the daily life of the Hummel children, promising completely new adventures.

A child in front of a cactus poses typical children's questions. But is this child really a child? Or is it the caricature of an adult before the mirror in the morning, experiencing the adventure of self-knowledge? The picture humorously leaves open the possibility of either interpretation.

> *"Doesn't scare me!*
> *Bein' scared's an art I don't seem to have learned."*

From a fairy tale About Someone Who Went Away to Learn About Fear

On the other Side
H 153

Whoever has too little trust
Is fearful everywhere;
Whoever has a surplus must
Ev'ry instant scare …

On Tiptoes
H 159

Behind the Fence
H 160

Feathered Friends
H 157

... A little fence keeps them apart,
The pair of troublemakers;
Too little or excess of heart,
makes them peacebreakers.

Wilhelm Busch

Bye-Bye!
H 210

Wayside Harmony
H 289

Just Resting
H 290

You ever come across surprise
In wholly unexpected guise.

Wilhelm Busch

Crossroads
H 615

The Fisherman
H 237

The earth's richest recompense
Is happy heart and common sense.

Johann Gottfried Seume

Sunflower Shade
H 108

Chicken-Licken
H 376

The Globetrotter
H 216

Happiness
H 268

*The second danger that they experienced
cannot, however, be compared with the first.*

Grimm's Fairy Tales, The Seven Swabings

The Skier
H 264

A Little Hare
H 374

The Unexpected Guest
H 112

If things're safe you want a fight;
When trouble comes you're out'a sight.

Grimm's Fairy Tales, The Seven Swabings

Adventure Bound
H 214

It used to be that everything
Kept merrily to its own place;
Darned hard it was to paint a thing
And if you could you were an ace. ...

Confidentially
H 254

The Toothache
H 257

Honey Lovers
H 116

... Now, discount your lacking skill and art,
Just set your camera up
And watch pictures from the box depart
Like little sparrows off to sup.

Wilhelm Busch

The Photographer
H 260

*Heidi sat up straight, next to Klara,
and read a story to her, obviously
with the greatest astonishment and
plunging with growing eagerness into
the new world ...*

Johanna Spyri: Heidi

Little Women and Little Men
With Lots to Do

Children Take Over Tasks in the World

When playing, children learn to identify with the adult world. Sometimes they can be uncommonly industrious and well-mannered. They enthusiastically act out the roles of adults: collect for the poor or write letters to Santa Claus, play at working or actually take over and carry out real tasks.

Children in the country who look after animals belong here, but there is also another group among the Hummel children which isn't dressed in alpine farmer's clothing. They could as well be living in a German or American city. An early and apt example is Goethe's Gretchen who describes how she, while but a child, took care of the house and did the laundry. Earlier, in the rearing of girls she played no small role as model. But doesn't one recognize still other figures from the children's literature of the nineteenth and twentieth centuries? Heidi is totally lost in her book but still knows how to be helpful in practical things. The friend of the "Little Lord" shows his gleaming polished shoes. From Louisa M. Alcott's novel "Little Women, Good Wives" come the three year old twins Demi and Daisy who might well be the inspiration for the little couple at table. Daisy sews and has a tiny kitchen. Demi learns the alphabet from grandfather and early on betrays a genius for engineering by inventing a wheel chair.

Today one asks oneself whether these children are not a bit too good, whether they don't in fact meet the expectations of adults a bit too readily and thereby shorten their childhood.

Whoever will good workers see
Will find they mostly children be.

Folk song

Little Boots
H 255

At three, Daisy demanded a "needler",
and actually made a bag with four stitches in it.

Louisa M. Alcott: Little Women, Good Wives

Mother's Helper
H 201

Demi learned his letters with his grandfather,
who invented a new mode of teaching the alphabet
by forming the letters with his arms and legs.

Louisa M. Alcott: Little Women, Good Wives

Little Bookkeeper
H 202

Worries are just awful guests,
Stick to you like most frightful pests.
On all you have to quickly turn your back;
For if you've got your work on track
You easily can give them the sack.

Otto Julius Bierbaum

The Little Sweeper
H 234

Big Housecleaning
H 173

Starting Young
H 189

Going to Grandma's
H 188

*And early morning sees me do the wash,
Do shopping and then get the cooking going,
The same always, pace never slowing.*

Gretchen, from: Goethe's Faust

Washday
H 232

You don't know the land
Where cannons bloom?
You truly don't?
You'll soon know all about it.

Erich Kästner

Head Up
And Swallow

Caricatures and
Commentaries on the Times

In the face of her mostly comic-idyllic scenes one forgets all too easily that the sensitive Berta Hummel in her student days had drawn drunks and scandal-mongers in the style of Simplizissimus caricatures and could effectively comment on the dark sides of life in her times. The artist perceived clearly how the Nazi dictators were governing.

"Beloved fatherland…" earned her hate-filled tirades in the Hitler press which attacked the "hydrocephalic creatures". Next the sale of Hummel figurines in Germany was restricted. Berta Hummel shared the fate of the "degenerate artists" and writers who, like Erich Kästner, were reduced to complete silence. Once when the Gestapo was searching the convent she showed her gallows humour by bringing out the drawing of the little duck hung on the door of the refectory to advise "Head up and swallow". The "Captive" picture shows the alternative. Hummel children never fit the master race type which had to be "hard as Krupp steel" and well combed like " Hitler youth Quex". Touchingly disheveled, as one expects children to be, the richly varied if artistically stylized faces fit no totalitarian pattern.

The chubby-cheeked physiognomy is reserved for caricature. Here Berta Hummel criticizes adults: the politically immature Hitler hangers-on, the heartless boss. Just compare the childish creatures of artistic caricature with the childlike intensity of the two girls earnestly painting. However, the howling singer or the stargazer who can't interpret the signs of the times show what a proportionately mild form of criticism it is to draw grownups as children.

No, the "beloved fatherland" can't remain calm when the nation's youth are being represented as dopey brats... There is no room among German artists for the likes of her!

Criticism of Hummel in the Magazine "Der SA-Mann" 1937

Volunteers
H 655

You don't know the land where cannons bloom?
You truly don't? You'll soon know all about it.
They talk there of war with no trace of gloom
And they won't stop with talk. Never doubt it. ...

The Boss
H 239

... There all are given a corporal's training
Invisible helms cap their attire.
Their looks but no intelligence retaining,
They hop into bed quite simply to sire....

At Your Service
H 233

There freedom has no home but just a tomb,
They build for soldiers and could do without it.
You don't know the land where cannons bloom?
You truly don't? You'll soon know all about it.

Erich Kästner: You don't know the land where cannons bloom? (1928)

Captive
H 200

... The fine and good things, as always, you're stacking
above the couch in an empty spot.
As always you seem to be fully lacking
a sense of the fitting and the not. ...

Latest News
H 245

Too Short to Read
H 247

The Conductor/I
H 248

The End of the Song
H 249

... You sprinkle sugar all over the achings
And think that underneath they cannot be.
You build once more for the heart's undertakings
And the thrashing soul you take on your knee.

Erich Kästner: And Have You Nothing Positive to Say, Mr. Kästner? (1930)

The Art Critic
H 252

The Artist
H 251

The Doctor
H 256

The Stargazer
H 242

You don't know the land? Most happy might it be!
Most happy be while happiness creating!
Minerals, coal and steel it has, and lea
Has strenght and zeal and beauty beyond stating...

Erich Kästner: You don't know the land where cannons bloom? (1928)

Hard Letters
H 622

Easy Letters
H 623

And suddenly there was with the angel a multitude of the heavenly army, praising God, and saying: Glory to God in the highest; and on earth peace to men of good will.

From: The Christmas Gospel according to St. Luke 2: 13-14

If Only There Were
Soon Peace

Variations on Old German
Calligraphy and Emblems

Usually, Berta Hummel's figures draw all attention to themselves, however, in one small group of pictures, script and symbol dominate. In them she continues in the best way the medieval tradition of ornate manuscripts with richly embellished letters to open chapters and the baroque art of emblems. The series is made up mostly of Christmas and New Year's motifs. To the sweeping opening letters she adds lively miniatures. The text on the other hand is set out in a simple, unornamented script "Glory to God in the highest and peace on earth to men ..."

Against the background of Nazi rule and the World War the Gospel for Christmas takes an added significance, and through her pictures the artist proclaims the old message of peace on earth to men of good will. Peace not only for Germans but also for Americans, French, British, Japanese ... Form is content, and the old German form employed by the artist evokes a time in which freedom was not in chains – evokes the old German dream of a "golden age" which the Romantics had dreamt.

Berta Hummel's great technical skill shows itself further when she brings medieval art form into line with modern taste and develops wordly motifs. Instead of letters, a symbol such as the heart can determine composition and content.

Another series is oriented toward the baroque art of symbols. The Christ Child and angels are painted as bearers of light and peace. Typical for the art of that epoch were globes and banners providing space whereon to write the Christian message.

Continue in the coming year
To shield us from all grief and fear,
And sickness, death and war beside
As God All-Merciful cast aside.

Good Whishes for the New Year (1612)

Good Luck in the New Year
H 488

O you most joyful, o you most blessed
You grace-filled days of Christmas-time!
We were all forlorn till the Lord was born
But now rejoice at this joyful time.

Johann Daniel Falk

Merry Christmas
H 483

Glory to God in the Highest
H 485

God is Born
H 493

Tomorrow children is the day
Tomorrow will we all rejoice!
We all will sing, we all will play
Resounding with a single voice.

Christmas carol

Love and Luck
H 484

Joyous Holidays
H 487

Bless Your Soul on Christmas
H 486

Whether in singing or complaining
Each has his things that he is bringing.
So push ahead without a tear
Take all into the bright New Year.

Saying on New Year

May You Sing
H 495

We Wish the Very Best
H 489

Blue Heart Baby
H 331

Red Heart Baby
H 332

Hosanna! Let all rejoice!
Sing out! Sing out without end.

Christmas anthem

Prince of Peace
H 482

Abide in My Love
H 680

Alleluja Angel
H 475

Jubilation
H 481

Praise to You my Lord
for Your entire creation,
Especially for the sun my sister
Who's day itself and through whom
You bring us light.
And she is lovely and shines
in wondrous splendor.

Francis of Assisi

Virgin and Child

Christian Motifs

Pictures of the Christ Child are among the oldest representations of children in western art. Often as with Dürer or da Vinci naked babies are depicted looking for all the world like real babies. Painter Berta Hummel doesn't leave the "Child in swaddling clothes" out of her work; however, she more often follows a model such as Murillo's "Holy Family" which shows Jesus about three years old with a bird. In her picture, composed in 1932-33, the form of the boy Jesus' head corresponds to that of children and angels created during the same period. Later religious pictures deliberately introduce distance. The reproach of "kitsch" with which the critics dismissed the postcard motifs should in no way be applied to the Divine Child. The physiognomy of Jesus accorded with the prevailing classical style.

Berta Hummel represents the Virgin and Child in different ways. At times Mary appears as a girl-like mother with child, scarcely distinguishable from other young mothers; at other times as radiant Queen of Heaven and powerful Lady of Perpetual Help. Such works show that Berta Hummel has taken from the most diverse styles and traditions – the "beautiful Ladies" of the late Gothic, Dürer's Christmas scenes, the women's heads of the Pre-raphaelites, and from the Orthodox their icons, whose halos glow in especially magnificent gold.

By the way, there exists a special type of the "pious" Hummel child. Wayside crosses and chapels to be found everywhere in Catholic Bavaria offer him the possibility of prayer and reflection as does the alpine landscape, God's creation.

O Mary you Queen of Heaven,
Set high above all the angels,
O root from which the Lord is sprung
Gate of light, your praise be sung.

Rottenburg Hymnal (1867)

Virgin Mother
H 539

You shine like the very sun,
O Mary, pure and bright —
From your beloved son,
Comes your wondrous light …

Mother of God
H 523

Mother of Christ
H 527

Mary Mother, Queen Maid
H 524

Trinity
H 471

... Remark her every feature,
The only perfect creature
The joy of all the world.

By Johann Khuen (1638)

Christ is Born
H 543

O Mary spread your lovely cloak,
Shelter and shield us like the oak ...

Mary Take Us into Your Care
H 531

*...: Let us there in safety stand
Till every storm has left the land.*

Hymn, Innsbruck (1640)

Resting
H 278

Prayer Time
H 276

In Full Harmony
H 383

Children on the Church Road
H 377

From my chest, do take the stone.
Angel, don't leave me alone.
Should all love leave me at last,
Let your arms still hold me fast.

Werner Bergengruen

In Guardian Arms

Angels in Heaven
and on Earth

In art it's traditional to represent angels as children. Countless cherubs abound in baroque and rococo Catholic churches and have become beloved figures of folk belief. At the same time the representation of children has been affected by such cherubs. The convent at Sießen has, thanks to Brother Zimmermann, some especially cheerful cherubs playing hide-and-seek among plaster curtains, just itching to be found. Berta Hummel also had a volume of reproductions by Fra Angelico whom she revered as an artist, and her angels and children are akin to his cherubs.

Child and angel in Berta Hummel's figures are often distinguished only by a pair of wings. The shape of head and body, joy in singing and love for animals are identical. Here the artist has not to create the distance from the child imposed by the canons for depicting a child Christ. The angel belongs as much to this world as to the Heavenly regions. Being a messenger, an angel may well, when delivering his message to a human being, sometimes wear ordinary human clothes.

When child and angel are shown together the angel is simply larger. He should and can protect the child. To do so is one of the main tasks of angels in the Bible. Raphael leads Tobias and even the Apostle Peter is spirited away from prison by an angel.

Angels have other important jobs too: to lead people along the true path by the light of their candles and lanterns, to play in the heavenly orchestra. The variety of instruments Hummel's angels have shows the influence of Fra Angelico.

Lord, we children know your love.
To each and all have you given
An angel sent down from heaven. ...

Deliver Us from Evil
H 402

He makes me think and understand;
While I'm at school, He's close at hand.
He helps me read and helps me write,
And keeps me ever in His sight.

From: Hummel's Little Prayer book

On the Way to School
H 701

Assistance
H 702

Sharing
H 703

Child's Prayer
H 704

Angel, you who watched while God
Set sun and moon and stars up there;
Maybe you do find odd
A child's delight just anywhere.

Clemens Brentano

A Gift for Jesus
H 626

Gift Bearers
H 624

While angels sing that God is here
"Gloria" sounds and resounds
from far and near.

Christmas carol (15th century)

Searching the Heavens
H 416

Trumpeting from Clouds
H 417

Christmas Tree Bearer
H 418

Angel/Light
H 414

Listen! Just hear the singing
And the bell's sweet ringing:
"O most holy night, reveal Christ to our sight."

Christmas carol

Heavenly Duo
H 415

Love is the one thing
That doesn't diminish
When we squander it.

Ricarda Huch

This
Is For You

For Birthdays, Valentine's Day
and All Days

Children are ambassadors. They bring messages from heart to heart, as does Cupid, god of love, often represented as a child. The Hummel children convincingly play the role of symbols of love perfectly suited to greeting cards for the most varied occasions.

Soon after Berta Hummel had composed something on the theme "Birthday" for her Art Academy entrance exam she began to supply the world with children as well-wishers on postcards. When her publisher Ars Sacra spread her work to America the question arose of what to offer the public there. It had to be taken into account that there were other days such as "Valentine's Day" to celebrate in America. Unsure what to make for America, Berta Hummel asked Maximiliane Müller for advice and was assured that she needed to paint nothing different for America. The language of children's gestures is understood everywhere.

Whom do the three little girls with flower pot, gingerbread heart and basket want to cheer up? Children do bring traditional gifts, but, when there are none of these, they bring much else that is absolutely priceless. A flower just picked, a song, the favorite toy, or themselves – like the little girl in the basket or the boy in the handwagon.

Whether they seem to come from the German fairy tale forest or from a modern city in the new world, they announce on feast days and ordinary days that love shared is not less, but more.

Love lives on lots of loving little things.

Theodor Fontane

Wee Three
H 357

Golden tones within my heart did slumber,
Golden tones I didn't remark …

Boys Ensemble
H 346

*... Now impulses of love without number
Hurl joyful ecstatic song from the dark.*

Theodor Storm

Girls Ensemble
H 347

And if you really love me, child,
Of these flowers, you get all, ...

The Birthday Gifts
H 283

... And at your window, for you to sing,
The nightingale will call.

Heinrich Heine

Quartet
H 284

To love and be loved in return
Is earth's most worthy prize to earn.

Achim von Arnim

Spring Basket
H 139

Take Me Along
H 337

Special Gift
H 348

Special Delivery
H 349

The love which loves from the heart
Is most rich and without art.

Emanuel Geibel

The Postman
H 246

What I see there, is just a cover.
The essential is invisible.

Antoine de Saint-Exupéry: The Little Prince

... A Few Small, Very Nice Things

Portraits of Children
and Late Works

From the beginning Berta Hummel's portraits have lighter colors than the usual children's pictures. For these she employed predominantly brown tones and autumn colors. In the works for America, at the request of her distributor, she again chose only two or three colors. In the posthumously released cycle "Last Gift" the children stand at last before a bright background and give the impression of being flooded with light.

This cycle was developed in 1946 during the last weeks of her life, when she, in a "passion for work", made another half dozen drafts for postcards. Modestly, she spoke of "a few small, very nice things". The girl with the doll, the flutist, the youngster with the umbrella and the girl with the basket are among them.

As a standard for successful pictures of children one could take Saint-Exupery's "Little Prince". He regarded the child as the most fragile of earth's precious things and considered what one saw as just a shell because he knew that "the essential is invisible." From an artistic standpoint it is a dangerous balancing act to make some of the essential visible and Berta Hummel knew that she didn't always succeed to the same degree. However, her portraits and no small number of her other representations of children do reveal the essential, the mysterious charm of the child who, in unspoiled innocence, is apparently able to see into and to love the whole world.

*Since the Little Prince had fallen asleep,
I took him into my arms.
To me it was as if I were carrying a fragile jewel.*

Antoine de Saint-Exupéry: The Little Prince

Sleepy Time
H 114

To forget and then to be forgot!
Everyone on earth has got
To admit that this be true,
To admit and then make do.

Theodor Storm

Rolf
H 185

Irmgard
H 186

Portrait of a Little Girl
H 136

First Portrait
H 135

The old is what you have forgot
The unforgettable's yesterday.
Forget the unforgettable not!

Erich Kästner: When I Was a Little Boy

Little Brother's Lesson
H 193

Create the best untiringly,
Addressing all inspiringly,
That's proven to bring joy at last.

Johann Wolfgang von Goethe

Teach Me to Fly
H 616

You don't measure by the clock but by the value.
And the most valuable, whether happy or sad,
is one's childhood.

Erich Kästner: When I Was a Little Boy

Springtime Joys
H 125

Acknowledgments

Literature:

Die andere Berta Hummel. Unbekannte Werke einer bekannten Künstlerin.
Ausstellung im Diözesanmuseum Obermünster Regensburg,
6. 11. 1986 – 1. 2. 1987 München, Zürich Schnell & Steiner, 1986.

50 Jahre „M. I. Hummel"-Figuren, 1935 – 1985, hrsg. vom Museum der Deutschen
Porzellanindustrie Hohenberg/Eger (Schriften und Kataloge des Museums der
Deutschen Porzellanindustrie Bd 5), Hohenberg/Eger 1985.

The Golden Anniversary Album. M. I. Hummel. New York, Toronto, London:
Portfolio Press Corporation, 1984.

Steinbichler, Josef: Berta Hummel – Ordensfrau und Künstlerin aus Massing.
In: Heimat an Rott und Inn, XII (1978).

Vierlinger, Rudolf: Berta Hummel, die berühmteste Simbacher Schülerin.
In: Heimat am Inn, 1982.

Wiegand, M. Gonsalva, OSF: "Sketch me, Berta Hummel!"
St. Meinrad (Ind.) USA 1949, 2. Aufl. 1951.

Photographs:
Page 4: The Hummel Museum, Inc., New Braunfels, Texas
Page 6: J. Hummel KG, Massing
Page 13: Luftbildverlag Hans Bertram, Haar
Page 14: The Hummel Museum, Inc., New Braunfels, Texas
Page 16: J. Hummel KG, Massing

Text Copyright:
The verse from Erich Kästner, "And Have You Nothing Positive to Say,
Mr. Kästner?", in: *Ein Mann gibt Auskunft,* 1930; from: "You Don't Know
the Land Where Cannons bloom?", in: *Herz auf Taille,* 1928, and *When I
Was a Little Boy* are printed with the permission of Atrium Verlag AG,
Zürich/Switzerland.

The reproduced portraits H 185 and H 186 on page 134 as well as H 174 on
page 79 belong to Robert L. Miller, Eaton/Ohio.
Most of the reproduced originals in this book are exhibited at the
Hummel Museum in New Braunfels/Texas.

Contents

Life and Work of Berta Hummel (1909-1946)
Page 5

What Is More Wonderful Than to Bring Joy to One's Fellowmen –
Early Pictures for Ars Sacra (1933-1934)
Page 25

Those Were Wonderful Days at Home – Life in the Country
Page 35

Hansel and Gretel –
Children Straight from Fairy Land
Page 47

Good Weather and Bad Weather – Children's Games
Page 55

Adventure Bound –
Exciting Experiences and Dangers in Everyday Life
Page 67

Little Women and Little Men With Lots to Do –
Children Take Over Tasks in the World
Page 79

Head Up And Swallow –
Caricatures and Commentaries on the Times
Page 87

If Only There Were Soon Peace –
Variations on Old German Calligraphy and Emblems
Page 97

Virgin and Child – Christian Motifs
Page 105

In Guardian Arms –
Angels in Heaven and On Earth
Page 113

This Is For You –
For Birthdays, Valentine's Day and All Days
Page 121

... A Few Small, Very Nice Things –
Portraits of Children and Late Works
Page 131

Acknowledgments
Page 138